When I Was Young

SHOPPING
IN THE 1940s

When I Was Young

SHOPPING
IN THE 1940s

Rebecca Hunter with Angela Davies

Evans

First published in this edition in 2012 by Evans Brothers Ltd
2A Portman Mansions
Chiltern St
London W1U 6NR

www.evansbooks.co.uk

British Library Cataloguing in Publication Data

Hunter, Rebecca, 1935-
Shopping in the 1940s. — (When I was young)
1. Davies, Angela—Childhood and youth—Juvenile literature. 2. Shopping—Great Britain—History—20th century—Juvenile literature. 3. Nineteen forties—Juvenile literature. 4. Great Britain—Social life and customs—1918-1945—Juvenile literature.
I. Title II. Series III. Davies, Angela, 1935-
381.1'0941'09044-dc22

ISBN-13: 9780237543891

Acknowledgements
Planning and production by Discovery Books Limited
Edited by Rebecca Hunter
Designed by Calcium

The publisher would like to thank Angela Davies and Kathleen Wood for their help in the preparation of this book, and The Collector's Gallery, Shrewsbury for the loan of the coins and notes on pages 12 and 13.

For permission to reproduce copyright material, the author and publishers gratefully acknowledge the following: The Advertising Archive Limited: 15 (middle), 18 (right); Hulton Getty: cover, 9, 10, 11, 14, 18 (left), 21, 22, 23, 25 (bottom), 27 (bottom), 28 (top); The Robert Opie Collection: 8 (top), 15, 17 (top, bottom); Derek Foxton 18, 19, 24, 26; The Frith Collection: 20; The Gloucester Collection: 27 (top).

Contents

'We lived above our general store.'

My name is Angela and I enjoy telling my family about my childhood. This photo shows me with Alice who is eleven and Fergus who is ten.

I was born in 1935 and grew up in a village called Burley Gate in Herefordshire. We lived above a post office and general store owned by my parents. My father was a coach driver and my mum ran the post office and shop.

Shops were very different in those days and I am going to tell you what shopping was like then.

'People queued at the counter.'

Our shop stood on a corner at the centre of the village. It was a red brick building with a white picket fence around it. There was a little bell on the door that rang when anyone came in. Inside there were shelves from floor to ceiling filled with packets, bottles, jars and tins.

Burley Gate Post Office and Police Station.

There was no self-service in those days and no carrier bags either. People brought their own bags or

baskets with them. They waited in a queue at the **grocery** counter until it was their turn to be served. Then they told you what they wanted and you went and fetched it for them.

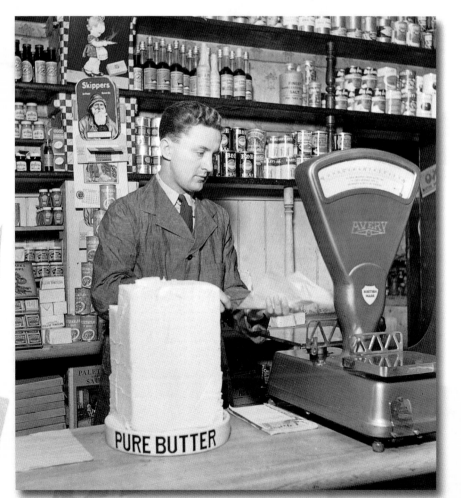

On one side of the shop was a marble-topped table where we sliced and weighed huge blocks of butter and whole cheeses.

PURE BUTTER

'The bread was still warm.'

Villages today usually have just one shop, or sometimes no shops at all. When I was a girl, the bigger villages had lots of shops.

The village baker baked his own bread on the premises. Some people had it delivered to their homes by bicycle.

It was often still warm when it arrived at our house!

Butchers wore stripy aprons and laid out their produce on marble slabs in the window. Salted and fresh meat hung on hooks, often outside the shop.

The village greengrocer had all his fruit and vegetables set up outside the shop. He would tip your vegetables straight into your basket.

No one had refrigerators to keep food fresh in those days, so shopping had to be done every day.

'We had pounds, shillings and pence.'

Money was different in those days. Instead of pounds and pence like today, we had pounds, shillings and pence. There were twelve pence (12d) to the shilling, and twenty **shillings** (20/-) to the pound (£1). A ha'penny was half a penny and a farthing was half a ha'penny. A two-shilling coin was called a florin and two shillings and sixpence (2/6) was half a crown.

We had many more types of coins and bank notes. You could get a one pound note and a ten shilling note. This would be like having a 50p note nowadays!

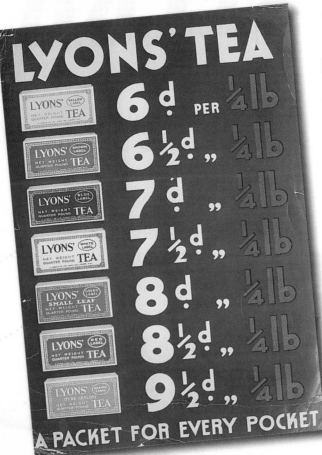

Food cost a lot less.
A loaf of bread would
cost about four pence
ha'penny (4½d) which is
worth about 2p today,
and a small bun would
be a penny farthing
(1¼d), less than
1p now!

'Food was not wrapped in plastic.'

I helped in the shop in the evenings and at weekends. Food in those days was not wrapped in plastic and packaged in cardboard; everything had to be weighed out separately. Things were weighed in **pounds** (lbs) and **ounces** (oz) then, not kilograms and grams like today.

Biscuits were sold loose from 7lb tins. Flour and sugar arrived in large cloth sacks which stood on the floor. Using a small metal scoop, I would weigh out the amount required and put it in coloured paper bags: white for flour and blue for sugar.

I particularly enjoyed serving sweets to my friends. The most popular were Sherbert Fountains, which cost a ha'penny. Mars bars were more expensive and cost threepence ha'penny.

'Shopping took much longer.'

Sometimes we would go shopping in Hereford, our local town.

Shopping in town was very different then. There were many small shops and few big stores. Shopping took much longer because lots of different shops had to be visited.

Many of today's large **chain stores** such as Debenhams, Boots and Marks and Spencer existed but they were tiny compared to now and sold far fewer things.

Hereford also had a W H Smith and my mum belonged to their private library. While she was choosing her books, I would look at the comics, deciding which one to buy with my pocket money. I usually got *Chick's Own* or *Sunny Stories*.

'Many people made their own clothes.'

In those days there were fewer clothing shops than there are today and clothes were expensive. So many people bought material and paper patterns to make their own clothes at home.

Occasionally we went into town to buy material for my clothes. At the **drapers** my mum would choose a pattern and I was allowed to choose the material.

We also bought shoes in town. There weren't so many to choose from then. Some shoe shops had machines called pedoscopes which took x-rays of your feet to see how well your shoes fitted. A few years later doctors realised x-rays could damage your bones if used too often and so pedoscopes were banned.

'Market day in Hereford.'

Wednesday was market day in Hereford. All the farmers brought their **livestock** and **produce** to the market on this day. My mum closed the shop in the afternoon, so that she could go to the market. During the school holidays, I looked forward to Wednesdays, when I could go to market too.

I enjoyed wandering among the pens in the livestock market, hearing the farmers haggle over the price of a pair of pigs or a flock of sheep.

My mum was not interested in the animals. She wanted to wander round the market square looking at all the brightly coloured stalls. She enjoyed looking at the clothing stalls and bought fresh fruit and vegetables from the farmers' wives.

'Everybody had a ration book.'

During and after the Second World War, food was **rationed**. Everybody had a ration book with **coupons** which showed how much of each type of food they were allowed per week. Bacon, butter, cheese, sugar and sweets were some of the rationed foods that our shop sold. These had to be carefully measured out.

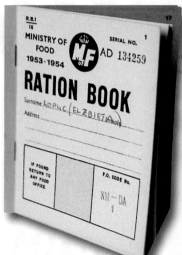

Children under five years old had green ration books. I thought it was very unfair when bananas arrived in the shops and were only available to green ration book customers!

Every Saturday evening we had to count up the ration coupons we had received that week. My mum could only buy more stock for the shop with the coupons she had been given by the customers, so we were very careful not to lose any.

'Mum had a mobile shop.'

Many shops had delivery vans so they could deliver goods to people who lived in the smaller **hamlets**. Here is a baker's van from Hereford delivering bread to a remote farmhouse.

My mum had an old ambulance that had been made into a mobile shop. She used it in September to deliver food to the hop-pickers. Hundreds of people came down from Birmingham to help pick the hops. Whole families would live in a barn on the farm, sleeping on the hay and cooking on camp fires. My mum would sell them food and supplies from her mobile shop in the evenings.

Sometimes I was allowed to go and help with the hop-picking. We got paid by the **bushel**. I used the money I earned to save up for a bicycle that cost £10.

'Department stores were magical.'

As a Christmas treat we would go shopping in Gloucester. This was an exciting journey as we had to go by train. There were far more shops in Gloucester and they were much bigger than those in Hereford, with a better selection of goods.

My favourite was the **department store** Bon Marche. I loved to travel in the lift, although my mum was always worried I would get my fingers caught in the metal doors!

At each floor the lift attendant would call out the floor number and what was sold on that floor. 'First floor **haberdashery** and shoes - going up.'

Department stores were magical places to me, I had never seen so many wonderful things as in the toy department at Christmas time!

'Shopping began to change.'

In the 1950s the first self-service supermarkets were introduced and shopping began to change.

Today supermarkets and shopping centres are so large that they have to be built on the edges of towns.

Many small village shops have closed since I was a child, but I am glad to say that our shop is still running as a post office. Here is a picture of it as it looks today with its present owner Mrs Hughes.

Glossary

Bushel A measurement of volume for corn or fruit.

Chain stores A series of shops owned by the same company.

Coupons Detachable tickets allowing you to buy a certain amount of food or clothing.

Department store A large shop with many different departments.

Drapers A shop selling clothing fabric.

Groceries Foods and general household goods.

Haberdashery Small items of clothing and fabric.

Hamlet A group of houses: smaller than a village.

Livestock Animals kept by farmers.

Ounces (oz) A unit of weight: 1 ounce = 28 grams.

Pounds (lbs) A unit of weight: 1lb = 0.45 kilogram.

Produce Fruit and vegetables grown for sale.

Rationing Limiting the amount of food and clothing that a person is allowed to buy.

Shilling A coin worth twelve old pence.

Useful books and websites

There are lots of books to read and websites to visit to learn more about shopping in the 1940s. Here are a few to get you started:

www.bbc.co.uk/schools/primaryhistory/world_war2/food_and_shopping/
Read about food and shopping, with fun activities and quizzes. Click on 'Rationing – shop for a meal in 1943', and have a go at shopping for dinner.

www.1900s.org.uk/1940s-edgware-shopping.htm
Read about shopping in the 1940s.

www.nationalarchives.gov.uk/education/homefront/life/rationing/default.htm
Interactive website with activities, worksheets and timelines.

Food and Rations (In the War), Peter Hicks, Wayland 2010

Rationing (At Home in World War Two), Stewart Ross, Evans 2007

Rationing (Britain at War), Martin Parsons, Wayland 2004

Activities and cross-curricular work

Activities suggested on this page support progression in learning by consolidating and developing ideas from the book and helping the children to link the new concepts with their own experiences. Making these links is crucial in helping young children to engage with learning and to become lifelong learners.

Ideas on the next page develop essential skills for learning by suggesting ways of making links across the curriculum and in particular to literacy, numeracy and ICT.

Word Panel

Check that the children know the meaning of each of these words and ideas from the book, in addition to the words in the glossary.

- Afterwards
- Ago
- Baker, butcher, draper, greengrocer
- Before
- Carrier bag
- General store
- Grocery counter
- Hops, hop-picker
- Marble-topped table
- Market
- Picket fence
- Refrigerator
- Self-service

Research Questions

Once you have read and discussed the book, ask groups of children to talk together and think of more information they would like to know. Can they suggest where to look for the answers?

Your High Street

Discuss how we know about things that happened in the past where you live.

- Do a mini-project on your high street.
- Begin by taking children on a local history walk in the high street, helping them to look for signs that would tell them about the age of a property. If they're looking at shops in older buildings, look above the plate glass windows to the windows and chimneys above.
- Let them sketch or photograph some of the buildings that might have been there in the 1940s.

- Visit local museums and libraries to find books and photographs about your high street in the past.
- Go to the offices or website of the local newspaper to find photographs and articles about the high street. Readers often send in photographs.
- Use the images and drawings you have to construct a display of what the area looked like 60 years ago.
- Ask an older resident who has lived in the community for most of their life to talk about their memories of the place.
- Talk about why things might have changed.

Change

Ask children to research the impact on the environment, as well as on lifestyle, of changes to the way in which we shop for food. Consider, for example:

- The distance some of the goods have travelled, but the increase in customer choice.
- The use of fields to build huge supermarkets but the time it takes to shop in many shops rather than just one.
- The use of plastic for wrapping and carrying food but the protection the wrapping gives.

Recreating old shops

Challenge children to use large cardboard boxes to recreate old shops or complete a design project showing the different aspects in drawing and photographs. Children will need to:

- Research what the interiors of the shops might have looked like.
- Construct shelving, tables, cupboards, service counters etc in their 'shop'.
- Find objects to 'dress up' as products available in the 1940s.
- Research packaging to populate their shelves.

Some children may prefer to consider what they have learned about change in shopping habits and construct shops of the future. What will they look like? What kinds of produce will they contain?

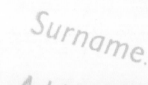

Using 'Shopping in the 1940s' for cross-curricular work.

The web below indicates some areas for cross-curricular study. Others may well come from your own class's engagement with the ideas in the book.

The activities suggested will help children to develop key competencies as:

- successful learners
- confident individuals and
- responsible citizens.

Cross-curricular work is particularly beneficial in developing the thinking and learning skills that contribute to building these competencies because it encourages children to make links, to transfer learning skills and to apply knowledge from one context to another. As importantly, cross-curricular work can help children to understand how school work links to their daily lives. For many children, this is a key motivation in becoming a learner.

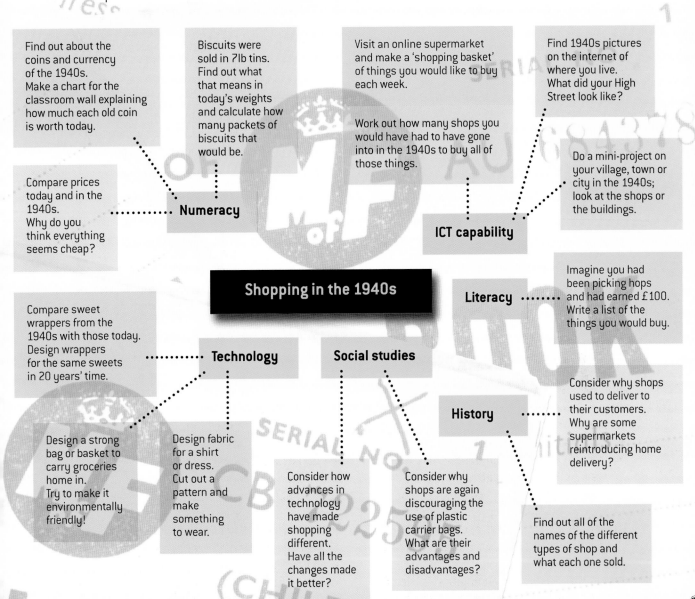

Find out about the coins and currency of the 1940s. Make a chart for the classroom wall explaining how much each old coin is worth today.

Biscuits were sold in 7lb tins. Find out what that means in today's weights and calculate how many packets of biscuits that would be.

Visit an online supermarket and make a 'shopping basket' of things you would like to buy each week.

Work out how many shops you would have had to have gone into in the 1940s to buy all of those things.

Find 1940s pictures on the internet of where you live. What did your High Street look like?

Compare prices today and in the 1940s. Why do you think everything seems cheap?

Numeracy

ICT capability

Do a mini-project on your village, town or city in the 1940s; look at the shops or the buildings.

Shopping in the 1940s

Literacy

Imagine you had been picking hops and had earned £100. Write a list of the things you would buy.

Compare sweet wrappers from the 1940s with those today. Design wrappers for the same sweets in 20 years' time.

Technology

Social studies

History

Consider why shops used to deliver to their customers. Why are some supermarkets reintroducing home delivery?

Design a strong bag or basket to carry groceries home in. Try to make it environmentally friendly!

Design fabric for a shirt or dress. Cut out a pattern and make something to wear.

Consider how advances in technology have made shopping different. Have all the changes made it better?

Consider why shops are again discouraging the use of plastic carrier bags. What are their advantages and disadvantages?

Find out all of the names of the different types of shop and what each one sold.

Key Successful learners   Confident individuals   Responsible citizens

Index